Guenther Steiner

In the picturesque town of Merano, nestled in the breathtaking South Tyrol region of Italy, a young Guenther Steiner came into the world on April 7, 1965. Little did anyone know that this son of a butcher would grow up to become a prominent figure in the world of motorsports, leaving an indelible mark on the Formula One stage.

From an early age, Steiner exhibited a passion for engineering, setting the stage for a remarkable journey ahead. Although he embarked on a path of engineering studies, fate had different plans for him. Without completing his degree, Steiner found himself drawn to Belgium, where his career in motorsports would take root.

The World Rally Championship became Steiner's training ground from 1986 to 1988, as he served as a mechanic for the Mazda Rally Team Europe. His skills and dedication did not go unnoticed, leading to a series of roles that would define his early career. From being the assistant team manager for Top Run Srl to head of reconnaissance and technical manager at Jolly Club, Steiner steadily climbed the ranks in the rallying world.

In 1997, he took the helm at Prodrive's Allstar Rally team, securing victory in the European Rally Championship. His journey continued with M-Sport in 1998, where he played a pivotal role as project manager, ultimately achieving consecutive runner-up finishes in the 2000 and 2001 seasons with the Ford World Rally Team.

The allure of Formula One beckoned, and in 2001, Steiner transitioned to the pinnacle of motorsports when he assumed the role of team principal at Jaguar Racing. Despite challenges and underperformance in the 2002 season, Steiner's organizational skills and cost-cutting measures were evident. However, the winds of change swept through the team, leading to his departure in 2003.

Red Bull Racing became the next chapter in Steiner's F1 journey. His tenure from 2005 to 2008 saw him contribute to the team's success alongside team principal Christian Horner. The call of new challenges led Steiner to the United States, where he served as Team Red Bull's technical director in the world of NASCAR from April 2006 to April 2008.

Steiner's story took an entrepreneurial turn when he founded Fibreworks Composites in 2009. However, it was a chance encounter with Joe Custer and Gene Haas that set the stage for his most significant venture. Over a steak dinner, Steiner proposed the idea of Haas F1 Team, an American entry into Formula One. With determination and meticulous planning, he became the team principal when Haas entered the grid in 2016, marking the first American constructor in 30 years.

Under Steiner's guidance, Haas F1 Team made an impressive debut, scoring points in their first race and finishing 8th in the constructor standings for the season. This achievement solidified Steiner's reputation as a capable leader and visionary in the highly competitive world of Formula One.

Beyond the racetrack, Steiner's personal life adds depth to his narrative. Holding both Italian and American passports, he resides in Mooresville, North Carolina, with his wife, Gertraud, and their daughter. Fluent in German, Italian, and English, Steiner embodies the multicultural spirit that enriches the Formula One community.

As the current team principal of the Haas Formula One Team, Guenther Steiner continues to navigate the twists and turns of the F1 landscape, leaving an enduring legacy as a determined, innovative, and resilient figure in the world of motorsports.

Beyond the racetrack, Guenther Steiner's personal and professional life intertwines, creating a narrative as dynamic as the Formula One races he orchestrates. As he made Mooresville, North Carolina, his home after leaving Red Bull Racing, Steiner's entrepreneurial spirit blossomed with the founding of Fibreworks Composites in 2009.

While the US F1 Team was still in the conceptual phase, fate intervened at a steakhouse where Steiner met Joe Custer and Gene Haas of Stewart-Haas Racing. Though they initially declined to invest in the F1 project, Steiner's proposal to enter the sport by ordering a customer car sparked their interest. When delays in securing approval arose, the trio decided to apply for entry as a privateer team, and thus, the Haas F1 Team was born.

Described as "the prime 'doer'" by motorsport publication Autosport, Steiner took charge, handpicking the core team, personally interviewing every member, and forging crucial partnerships with renowned entities like Dallara and Ferrari. On April 14, 2014, his role as the official team principal of the Haas F1 Team was announced, marking a historic moment as the team prepared to enter the 2016 Formula One season.

With Haas F1 Team's debut, Steiner orchestrated a spectacle that hadn't been seen in decades – the return of an American constructor to Formula One. The 2016 Australian Grand Prix became a milestone as Romain Grosjean, behind the wheel of the Haas car, secured a remarkable 6th-place finish, earning eight points and setting a precedent for success.

As the season unfolded, Haas F1 Team continued to make waves, finishing 8th in the constructor standings with 29 points, all scored by Grosjean. Steiner's strategic vision, coupled with his ability to navigate the complexities of Formula One, propelled Haas into the spotlight.

Steiner's leadership style became synonymous with resilience and adaptability, traits that were crucial in the competitive world of Formula One. His journey, marked by highs and lows, showcased not only his technical acumen but also his capacity to inspire and lead a team toward success.

In the realm of personal life, Steiner, holding both Italian and American passports, found a haven in Mooresville with his wife, Gertraud, and their daughter. Fluent in German, Italian, and English, Steiner exemplifies the cosmopolitan nature of Formula One, a sport that transcends borders and cultures.

As the Haas F1 Team continues its journey under Steiner's guidance, the motorsport world eagerly awaits the next chapter in this compelling story. Guenther Steiner, the Italian-American force shaping the destiny of Haas, stands not only as a team principal but as a testament to determination, vision, and the pursuit of excellence on the Formula One stage. The twists and turns of the racetrack mirror the twists and turns of his life, creating a narrative that is as thrilling as the races he orchestrates.

In the ever-evolving saga of Guenther Steiner's life, the chapters beyond the inaugural season of Haas F1 Team unveil a tale of perseverance, strategic brilliance, and a relentless pursuit of excellence. As the team principal, Steiner faced the challenges of the highly competitive Formula One landscape with unwavering determination.

The 2017 and 2018 seasons saw Haas F1 Team solidify its presence in the sport, with Steiner at the helm steering the team through the intricacies of car development, race strategies, and the constant quest for improvement. Despite the hurdles that every Formula One team encounters, Steiner's leadership remained resolute, guiding Haas to consistent performances on the global stage.

In 2018, Haas F1 Team reached a significant milestone as they finished fifth in the constructor standings, a testament to Steiner's strategic decisions and the team's collective efforts. It was a moment of triumph, showcasing the progress made since their debut just two years earlier. Steiner's adept management style had not only established Haas as a competitive force but had also garnered respect from the Formula One community.

However, the journey in Formula One is a relentless pursuit of perfection, and the subsequent seasons brought new challenges for Steiner and his team. The highs and lows on the racetrack mirrored the ebb and flow of the team's fortunes, yet through it all, Steiner's commitment to the pursuit of excellence never wavered.

Off the track, Steiner's role extended beyond the technical and strategic aspects of Formula One. He became a prominent figure in media interactions, known for his candid and straightforward demeanor. Steiner's interviews and behind-the-scenes glimpses provided fans with insights into the complexities of running a Formula One team, further establishing a connection between Haas F1 Team and its global fanbase.

As the seasons unfolded, Haas F1 Team continued to evolve under Steiner's watchful eye. New drivers, technical innovations, and strategic partnerships contributed to the team's narrative, creating a story that resonated with Formula One enthusiasts around the world. Steiner's ability to adapt to the ever-changing dynamics of the sport showcased his versatility and resilience as a leader.

The personal and professional dimensions of Steiner's life remained intertwined. The camaraderie within the team extended beyond the paddock, forging bonds that withstood the challenges of a rigorous Formula One calendar. Steiner's family, too, remained a pillar of support, providing a sense of stability amid the dynamic and demanding world of motorsports.

As we stand on the brink of the present day, the next chapters of Guenther Steiner's journey in Formula One remain unwritten. The racetrack echoes with the roar of engines, and the twists and turns continue to shape the destiny of Haas F1 Team. Through victories and defeats, challenges and triumphs, Guenther Steiner remains at the heart of this narrative, a driving force in the relentless pursuit of Formula One glory.

As the calendar pages turned and the Formula One seasons progressed, Guenther Steiner's story continued to unfold, each race adding a new layer to the tapestry of his career. The 2019 and 2020 seasons brought both excitement and challenges for Haas F1 Team under Steiner's stewardship.

During these years, Steiner navigated the intricate dance of competition, team dynamics, and technical advancements. The ever-changing Formula One regulations posed constant challenges, requiring adaptability and innovation. Despite the ups and downs, Steiner's strategic mindset and commitment to pushing the boundaries of performance persisted.

One of the defining moments came in 2019 when Haas faced a mid-season slump. Steiner, undeterred, led the team through a process of introspection and refinement. The ability to identify weaknesses and implement changes showcased Steiner's resilience and determination. It was a testament to his leadership style—bold, decisive, and focused on continuous improvement.

As the world grappled with unprecedented challenges in 2020, the Formula One circus adapted to a new normal. Steiner's role expanded to include managing the complexities arising from the global pandemic. Navigating logistical hurdles, ensuring the well-being of the team, and keeping the competitive spirit alive required a unique set of skills, ones that Steiner exhibited with grace.

Off the track, Steiner's visibility in the media landscape continued to grow. His candid interviews and interactions became a staple, endearing him to fans who appreciated his unfiltered insights into the inner workings of Formula One. Steiner's ability to balance the demands of the media with the responsibilities of leading a competitive team added a human touch to the often high-stakes world of racing.

As the seasons unfolded, Haas F1 Team introduced new talent into their driver lineup, reflecting Steiner's commitment to nurturing young talent and building a team for the future. The roster changes, coupled with technical advancements, hinted at a strategic vision that extended beyond immediate challenges, laying the groundwork for sustained success.

Beyond the paddock, Steiner's influence in Mooresville and the broader motorsport community grew. His endeavors, from Fibreworks Composites to the establishment of Haas F1 Team, marked him not only as a seasoned motorsport professional but also as a visionary entrepreneur with a passion for innovation.

The most recent chapters in Steiner's biography underscore a life dedicated to the pursuit of excellence, both on and off the track. The roaring engines, the tire-squealing turns, and the adrenaline-fueled drama of Formula One continue to be the backdrop of Steiner's journey—a journey marked by victories, setbacks, and an unwavering commitment to the relentless pursuit of success.

As we step into the current day, the story of Guenther Steiner is a living testament to the dynamism of motorsports, the resilience of the human spirit, and the enduring pursuit of greatness. The racetrack awaits, and with each lap, Steiner continues to etch his legacy into the annals of Formula One history.

In the latest chapters of Guenther Steiner's compelling biography, the pulse of Formula One beats with anticipation as Haas F1 Team continues to carve its path through the twists and turns of the racing world. The most recent seasons have been a testament to Steiner's ability to steer the team through the competitive storms that define the sport.

The 2021 and 2022 seasons brought fresh challenges and triumphs for Haas F1 Team. As Steiner fine-tuned the team's strategy, the dynamic nature of Formula One once again demanded adaptability. New regulations, technological advancements, and the ever-present pursuit of speed propelled Haas into the heart of the racing narrative.

Steiner's leadership style, characterized by a delicate balance of pragmatism and ambition, guided the team through pivotal moments. The grid witnessed emerging talents under the Haas banner, a reflection of Steiner's commitment to fostering a new generation of drivers. As the team refined its competitive edge, Steiner's vision continued to extend beyond the immediate races, outlining a roadmap for sustained success.

The media spotlight remained firmly on Steiner, whose candid interviews and transparent communication style continued to resonate with fans. In an era where Formula One transcends the racetrack, becoming a global spectacle, Steiner's role as the face of Haas F1 Team contributed to the team's narrative both on and off the circuit.

The Haas F1 Team's journey mirrored the broader trends in the world of motorsports. The quest for sustainability, innovation, and inclusivity became integral themes, and Steiner positioned Haas at the forefront of these conversations. Whether discussing technical developments, team dynamics, or the future landscape of Formula One, Steiner's insights reflected a deep understanding of the sport's evolution.

The personal and professional spheres of Steiner's life continued to intersect. His family, a source of strength and support, remained steadfast as he navigated the high-speed, high-stakes world of Formula One. The town of Mooresville, where Steiner established his base, became a hub of motorsport innovation, reflecting his lasting impact on the community.

As we stand at the intersection of the past and the present, the chapters of Guenther Steiner's biography unfold with a sense of anticipation. The racetrack remains a proving ground, each lap a canvas for the team principal to paint a story of determination, strategy, and the pursuit of victory.

The story of Guenther Steiner is far from concluded, and the upcoming seasons hold the promise of new challenges, triumphs, and milestones. The roar of engines, the scent of burning rubber, and the cheers of fans are the backdrop to Steiner's ongoing journey—an odyssey that transcends the boundaries of sport, encapsulating the essence of resilience, innovation, and the relentless pursuit of excellence.

As the calendar turns to the present day, Guenther Steiner's narrative in the world of Formula One continues to evolve, each race weekend unfolding as a new chapter in his storied career. The recent seasons have seen Haas F1 Team navigating the intricate balance between performance, resource management, and the ever-shifting landscape of international motorsport.

The 2023 season dawned with a renewed sense of optimism and determination for Steiner and his team. The off-season brought changes, innovations, and a reshuffling of strategies as Haas aimed to climb further up the competitive ladder. Steiner's role as a strategic architect became increasingly pivotal, guiding the team through the complexities of Formula One's technological advancements and regulatory shifts.

In the midst of aerodynamic upgrades, tire strategies, and the relentless pursuit of speed, Steiner's leadership style continued to leave an indelible mark on Haas F1 Team. His ability to inspire and steer his team through both triumphs and setbacks solidified his reputation as one of the sport's preeminent leaders.

Off the track, Steiner's influence expanded beyond the paddock. His commitment to sustainability initiatives, technological innovation, and the development of young talent echoed a broader vision for the future of motorsport. As Formula One embraced a new era, Steiner played a key role in shaping Haas F1 Team's identity within this evolving landscape.

As the calendar turns to the present day, Guenther Steiner's narrative in the world of Formula One continues to evolve, each race weekend unfolding as a new chapter in his storied career. The recent seasons have seen Haas F1 Team navigating the intricate balance between performance, resource management, and the ever-shifting landscape of international motorsport.

The 2023 season dawned with a renewed sense of optimism and determination for Steiner and his team. The off-season brought changes, innovations, and a reshuffling of strategies as Haas aimed to climb further up the competitive ladder. Steiner's role as a strategic architect became increasingly pivotal, guiding the team through the complexities of Formula One's technological advancements and regulatory shifts.

In the midst of aerodynamic upgrades, tire strategies, and the relentless pursuit of speed, Steiner's leadership style continued to leave an indelible mark on Haas F1 Team. His ability to inspire and steer his team through both triumphs and setbacks solidified his reputation as one of the sport's preeminent leaders.

Off the track, Steiner's influence expanded beyond the paddock. His commitment to sustainability initiatives, technological innovation, and the development of young talent echoed a broader vision for the future of motorsport. As Formula One embraced a new era, Steiner played a key role in shaping Haas F1 Team's identity within this evolving landscape.

Media interactions remained a significant part of Steiner's routine. His candid interviews, often peppered with humor and genuine insights, provided fans with a window into the strategic mind behind Haas. The connection between the team and its global fanbase strengthened, transcending geographical boundaries and making Haas F1 Team a truly international sensation.

Mooresville, North Carolina, where Steiner chose to make his home, continued to serve as a hub of innovation. Beyond the roar of engines and the meticulous planning for race weekends, Steiner's impact on the local community grew, symbolizing the intersection of motorsport excellence and community engagement.

As Steiner navigates the challenges and triumphs of the contemporary Formula One landscape, his story becomes more than just a tale of a team principal. It's a testament to the enduring spirit of motorsport, where passion, innovation, and resilience converge on the global stage. The chapters that are being written today will become the foundation for the legacy of Guenther Steiner in the annals of Formula One history.

And so, with each passing race, the saga of Guenther Steiner unfolds, a dynamic narrative fueled by the burning desire to conquer new horizons. The twists and turns of the racetrack mirror the unpredictable journey of his life, a life intertwined with the high-speed drama of Formula One. As the checkered flag waves, signaling the end of one chapter and the beginning of the next, the legacy of Guenther Steiner remains a testament to the relentless pursuit of excellence in the world's most prestigious motorsport arena.

In the ongoing chronicle of Guenther Steiner's journey, the Formula One seasons continue to unfurl with their characteristic blend of drama, speed, and unpredictability. As Haas F1 Team ventures into new territories, Steiner's strategic prowess and resilience remain at the forefront of the team's narrative.

The 2023 season marks a pivotal moment in Steiner's career, a season where Haas F1 Team aims to break new ground and challenge the established order. With a renewed focus on technical innovation, driver development, and sustainability, Steiner's multifaceted approach underscores his commitment to shaping the future of the team and the sport.

As Haas drivers push the limits on circuits around the globe, Steiner's meticulous planning and decision-making come to the fore. The strategic chess game that is Formula One requires not only speed on the track but also astute maneuvers behind the scenes. Steiner's ability to navigate the intricacies of the sport positions Haas as a formidable contender in the ever-evolving Formula One landscape.

Off the track, Steiner's impact extends beyond the confines of the racing world. Embracing sustainability initiatives, the team under Steiner's guidance becomes a driving force for positive change. Whether it's adopting eco-friendly technologies or promoting environmental awareness, Haas F1 Team aligns with Steiner's vision for a more sustainable and responsible future.

Media engagements continue to be a dynamic aspect of Steiner's role. His authentic and transparent communication style resonates with fans, providing them with a unique glimpse into the inner workings of a Formula One team. Steiner's interviews are not just about races and podium finishes; they're windows into the passion, challenges, and triumphs that define the journey of Haas F1 Team.

The town of Mooresville, where Steiner chose to establish his base, witnesses the fusion of motorsport innovation and community involvement. Steiner's commitment to both the local and global aspects of Formula One creates a legacy that transcends the boundaries of the racetrack. His influence in shaping Mooresville as a hub of motorsport excellence becomes a testament to the enduring impact of Steiner's vision.

As each race weekend unfolds, the storyline of Guenther Steiner becomes intertwined with the ebb and flow of Formula One. The pursuit of excellence, the thrill of competition, and the continuous quest for improvement propel Steiner and Haas F1 Team into the future. The saga of Guenther Steiner, now an integral part of the sport's tapestry, continues to evolve, leaving an indelible mark on the history of Formula One.

The checkered flag waves, signaling not just the end of a race but the continuation of a journey defined by passion, perseverance, and an unyielding commitment to the pursuit of greatness. As the engines roar and the world watches, the legacy of Guenther Steiner unfolds, chapter by chapter, in the captivating and ever-evolving narrative of Formula One.

In the latest installment of Guenther Steiner's Formula One odyssey, the story takes an intriguing turn as the seasons progress, each race weaving new threads into the tapestry of his illustrious career. The 2023 season, fraught with challenges and opportunities, unfolds as a pivotal chapter in the narrative of Haas F1 Team.

As the team principal, Steiner finds himself at the nexus of strategic decisions and calculated risks. The dynamic nature of Formula One demands continuous innovation, and Steiner's ability to steer Haas through the complexities of technical regulations and sporting dynamics becomes more critical than ever. The pursuit of a competitive edge, both on and off the track, defines Steiner's leadership philosophy.

In this era of Formula One, where the sport's global impact reaches unprecedented heights, Steiner's vision extends beyond the confines of the racetrack. Haas F1 Team becomes a symbol of innovation, embracing cutting-edge technologies and sustainable practices. Under Steiner's guidance, the team takes bold steps toward reducing its environmental footprint, aligning with the evolving values of the motorsport community.

Media engagements continue to be a dynamic facet of Steiner's role. His candid interviews, peppered with humor and genuine insights, resonate not only with seasoned motorsport enthusiasts but also with a new generation of fans. Steiner's communication style becomes a bridge connecting the team's inner workings with the diverse audience that follows the drama of Formula One.

Away from the spotlight of the racetrack, Mooresville remains a hub of motorsport excellence and community engagement. Steiner's influence permeates the town, where local initiatives and outreach programs further solidify the team's bond with its roots. The symbiotic relationship between Haas F1 Team and the community reflects Steiner's commitment to nurturing a positive legacy beyond the racing circuits.

The evolution of Haas F1 Team's driver lineup mirrors Steiner's dedication to talent development. As young drivers emerge under the team's banner, Steiner's mentorship becomes a driving force for the next generation of Formula One stars. The team's commitment to fostering emerging talent aligns with Steiner's belief in building a sustainable and successful future for Haas.

As the checkered flag falls at the end of each race, the legacy of Guenther Steiner continues to unfold. The racetrack remains a theater of dreams, a place where passion, strategy, and resilience converge. Steiner's journey, marked by triumphs and challenges, encapsulates the essence of Formula One—a sport that transcends competition and becomes a testament to the indomitable spirit of those who dare to push the limits.

The upcoming races hold the promise of new storylines, fresh challenges, and unforeseen triumphs. As Steiner navigates the twists and turns of the Formula One calendar, the chapters of his biography continue to be written, leaving an enduring imprint on the sport and inspiring generations to come. The roar of the engines echoes, signaling not just the pursuit of victory but the relentless pursuit of excellence in the ever-evolving world of Formula One.

As the Formula One seasons unfold, Guenther Steiner's narrative takes on new dimensions, each race adding layers to the compelling story of Haas F1 Team. The latter part of the 2023 season becomes a crucible for Steiner's strategic acumen and the team's resilience as they navigate the challenges of a fiercely competitive grid.

In the heart of the racing action, Steiner's decision-making prowess becomes even more pivotal. The intricate dance of tire strategies, technical developments, and in-race adaptations defines the team's pursuit of podiums and points. Steiner's ability to read the ebb and flow of each race contributes to Haas F1 Team's ongoing quest for success.

Beyond the racetrack, Haas F1 Team under Steiner's stewardship remains a beacon of innovation. The fusion of cutting-edge technologies and sustainable practices solidifies the team's position as a trailblazer in the motorsport world. Steiner's commitment to environmental responsibility resonates not only within the Formula One community but also with a global audience increasingly conscious of the impact of their favorite sports.

Media interactions continue to be a highlight of Steiner's engagement with fans and pundits alike. His candid and unfiltered commentary provides a unique perspective into the challenges and triumphs of managing a Formula One team. Steiner's interviews become a mirror reflecting the highs and lows of the team, forging a connection with supporters that extends beyond the duration of a race weekend.

Mooresville, North Carolina, witnesses the continued convergence of motorsport excellence and community involvement. Steiner's vision for Haas F1 Team as a catalyst for positive change becomes evident through local initiatives, educational programs, and partnerships that enhance the team's connection with its roots. The town evolves into more than just a base—it becomes a testament to Steiner's commitment to leaving a lasting legacy.

The development of young talent within Haas F1 Team becomes a cornerstone of Steiner's approach. As emerging drivers make their mark under his mentorship, the team's investment in the future takes center stage. Steiner's belief in the potential of fresh talent not only contributes to the team's competitiveness but also aligns with a broader vision for sustaining success in the long run.

As the checkered flag waves at each Grand Prix, the legacy of Guenther Steiner unfolds in real-time. The roar of the engines, the jubilation of victory, and the introspection after defeat—all become integral parts of a story that transcends the confines of Formula One. Steiner's journey becomes emblematic of the spirit of relentless pursuit, a reminder that in the world of racing, the pursuit of excellence is a continuous journey rather than a destination.

The seasons may change, but Steiner's determination to push the boundaries and lead Haas F1 Team to new heights remains unwavering. The future beckons, promising more thrilling races, unforeseen challenges, and opportunities for Steiner and his team to etch their names further into the annals of Formula One history.

As the Formula One calendar progresses, Guenther Steiner's journey through the racing world enters a new chapter, marked by the twists and turns of the evolving seasons. The latter part of the 2023 season unfolds with heightened intensity, as each Grand Prix becomes a crucible where Steiner's leadership and Haas F1 Team's mettle are tested.

In the midst of the championship battle, Steiner's strategic decisions gain prominence. The team's relentless pursuit of performance optimization, coupled with Steiner's ability to anticipate the ever-changing dynamics of the races, positions Haas F1 Team as a formidable contender on the grid. With eyes on podiums and championship points, every decision becomes critical, and Steiner's experience becomes an invaluable asset.

Off the track, Haas F1 Team's commitment to sustainability under Steiner's guidance deepens. The team becomes a pioneer in adopting eco-friendly practices, from energy-efficient technologies to responsible waste management. Steiner's vision for a greener future resonates with fans, sponsors, and partners alike, transforming Haas F1 Team into a symbol of environmental responsibility in the high-speed world of Formula One.

Media engagements continue to capture the essence of Steiner's role as the face of Haas F1 Team. His interviews, press conferences, and behind-the-scenes glimpses offer fans a window into the human side of Formula One. Steiner's candor and humor add a personal touch to the team's narrative, fostering a unique bond with supporters who share in the triumphs and tribulations of the racing season.

Mooresville, North Carolina, stands as a testament to Steiner's legacy beyond the racetrack. The town thrives as a motorsport hub, not only housing Haas F1 Team's operations but also serving as a platform for community engagement. Steiner's commitment to uplifting the local community through educational initiatives and partnerships reflects a broader ethos of giving back.

The nurturing of young talent within Haas F1 Team continues to be a hallmark of Steiner's leadership. As emerging drivers find their place in the world of Formula One, Steiner's mentorship becomes a guiding force. The team's dedication to talent development reinforces its role as a breeding ground for future racing stars, further solidifying Steiner's imprint on the sport's landscape.

As the checkered flag waves at each Grand Prix, the legacy of Guenther Steiner is etched into the ongoing story of Formula One. The roar of the engines echoes not just within the confines of the racetrack but resonates across the global motorsport community. Steiner's journey becomes an inspiring narrative, reminding all who witness it that the pursuit of excellence is not just a race to the finish line but a relentless journey of self-discovery and evolution.

As the upcoming seasons beckon, promising more thrilling races, unexpected challenges, and opportunities for triumph, Guenther Steiner and Haas F1 Team stand poised at the intersection of history and destiny. The chapters yet to be written will further illuminate the legacy of a man whose passion for racing transcends the boundaries of time and track.

In the unfolding saga of Guenther Steiner and Haas F1 Team, the latter part of the 2023 season continues to deliver moments of exhilaration and challenge. Each Grand Prix is a new chapter, written with the ink of high-speed drama and strategic brilliance, as Steiner navigates the complexities of Formula One's elite echelons.

With the championship still hanging in the balance, Steiner's strategic mind becomes the linchpin of Haas F1 Team's aspirations. Every pit stop, tire change, and tactical decision plays a pivotal role in determining the team's success on the track. Steiner's adept management weaves a narrative of precision, adaptability, and an unwavering commitment to success.

Off the track, the sustainability initiatives pioneered by Haas F1 Team under Steiner's leadership gain momentum. The team's commitment to reducing its environmental impact resonates with fans worldwide, fostering a sense of collective responsibility for the future of the sport. Haas F1 Team becomes a trailblazer, setting new standards for eco-consciousness in the high-octane world of Formula One.

Media interactions remain a cornerstone of Steiner's engagement with the public. His interviews and press conferences provide not only insights into the team's strategies but also glimpses of the person behind the team principal title. Steiner's ability to connect with fans on a personal level strengthens the bond between Haas F1 Team and its global audience.

Mooresville, North Carolina, continues to thrive as a center of motorsport excellence and community impact. Steiner's commitment to local initiatives, educational programs, and fostering a sense of pride within the town becomes a testament to the positive influence of Haas F1 Team beyond the racetrack. The team's success becomes intertwined with the community's spirit, creating a symbiotic relationship that reflects Steiner's vision of motorsport as a force for good.

The nurturing of young talent within Haas F1 Team reaches a crescendo as emerging drivers make significant contributions to the team's performance. Steiner's mentorship becomes a legacy in the making, with the team standing as a testament to his belief in the power of youth and the potential for greatness in the world of Formula One.

As the championship reaches its climax, the checkered flag at each race becomes not just a marker of victory or defeat but a symbol of the enduring legacy being forged by Guenther Steiner. The roar of the engines becomes a collective anthem, resonating with the dreams and aspirations of fans worldwide.

The upcoming seasons hold the promise of new narratives, unforeseen challenges, and the relentless pursuit of Formula One glory. Guenther Steiner, as the orchestrator of this high-speed drama, stands at the helm, steering Haas F1 Team towards a future that beckons with the allure of triumph and the perpetual quest for excellence. The story is far from over; it's a living, breathing testament to the indomitable spirit of motorsport and the legacy of one man's unwavering passion for racing.

Mooresville, North Carolina, resonates with the hum of engines and the pulse of a community united by motorsport. Steiner's commitment to local initiatives and community engagement becomes a blueprint for the positive impact a Formula One team can have beyond the racetrack. The town becomes synonymous with success, a living testament to Steiner's vision of motorsport as a catalyst for positive change.

The nurturing of young talent within Haas F1 Team reaches a crescendo as emerging drivers become pivotal in the championship campaign. Steiner's foresight in developing a roster of young and dynamic racers becomes a strategic masterstroke, reinforcing the team's commitment to sustainability and long-term success. The blend of experience and youthful vigor becomes Haas F1 Team's secret weapon in the pursuit of glory.

As the checkered flag waves in the final races of the 2023 season, the legacy of Guenther Steiner stands at the crossroads of achievement and aspiration. The roar of the engines becomes a crescendo, echoing not only through the racetracks but resonating in the hearts of fans globally. Steiner's journey, marked by resilience, innovation, and a relentless pursuit of excellence, becomes a beacon for aspiring racers and motorsport enthusiasts alike.

As the sun sets on one season, the dawn of the next beckons. The story of Guenther Steiner and Haas F1 Team continues, an ever-evolving narrative shaped by the thrill of the race, the strategic brilliance of its leader, and the collective heartbeat of a global fanbase. The chapters yet to be written hold the promise of new triumphs, fresh challenges, and the perpetuation of a legacy that transcends the boundaries of Formula One.

In the unfolding chapters of Guenther Steiner's Formula One odyssey, the 2023 season reaches its zenith, a climax of anticipation and culmination of efforts for Haas F1 Team. Every race becomes a make-or-break moment, and the championship aspirations hang in the balance. Steiner, the maestro orchestrating the team's campaign, is acutely aware that the difference between victory and defeat lies in the intricate dance of strategy, skill, and sheer determination.

As the races unfold, each Grand Prix becomes a gripping chapter in the saga of Haas F1 Team's pursuit of glory. Steiner's leadership is tested in the crucible of high-stakes competition, where split-second decisions can make the difference between podium celebrations and unfulfilled dreams. The tension on the track is palpable, and Steiner's strategic acumen is a guiding force, steering the team through the complexities of Formula One's elite echelons.

Off the track, Haas F1 Team's commitment to sustainability continues to resonate with fans and stakeholders alike. Steiner's vision for environmental responsibility is not just a talking point but a living, breathing ethos ingrained in the team's DNA. The roar of the hybrid engines echoes the team's pledge to drive positive change, setting a standard for future generations in motorsport.

Media engagements during this critical juncture are a delicate balance for Steiner. Each interview, press conference, and public appearance becomes an opportunity to communicate the team's narrative. The global audience hangs on every word, every nuance, as Steiner provides insights into the team's state of mind, strategies, and aspirations. Haas F1 Team becomes not just a contender on the track but a captivating storyline that transcends the boundaries of the paddock.

In Mooresville, North Carolina, the connection between the team and the community deepens. Steiner's vision for Haas F1 Team as a force for positive change materializes as local initiatives, educational programs, and community partnerships thrive. The town, once a backdrop to the team's operations, transforms into a vibrant testament to the impact of motorsport on local life.

The nurturing of young talent continues to pay dividends, with emerging drivers proving their mettle on the world stage. Steiner's foresight in building a roster of young and dynamic racers becomes a cornerstone of the team's success. The blend of experience and youthful exuberance becomes a potent formula, setting Haas F1 Team apart in the highly competitive field.

As the final races of the season unfold, the checkered flag waves not just over the racetrack but over a chapter in the annals of Guenther Steiner's career. The legacy being crafted in the heat of competition becomes a symbol of perseverance, innovation, and a relentless pursuit of greatness. The motorsport world watches, and as the engines fall silent at the season's end, the echoes of Steiner's journey reverberate, leaving an indelible mark on the heart of Formula One.

As the curtain falls on the 2023 season, the promise of new challenges and triumphs looms on the horizon. The story of Guenther Steiner and Haas F1 Team, an ever-evolving narrative of speed, strategy, and legacy, continues to captivate the imaginations of racing enthusiasts worldwide. The chapters that lie ahead hold the potential for new heights, defining not just the team but the very essence of Formula One's enduring allure.

In the aftermath of the climactic 2023 season, the echoes of Guenther Steiner's journey reverberate through the motorsport world. The checkered flag has fallen, and Haas F1 Team's performance, a tapestry woven with strategic brilliance, environmental consciousness, and the pursuit of young talent, has left an indelible mark on Formula One.

Steiner, the seasoned architect behind Haas F1 Team's campaign, now finds himself at the crossroads of reflection and anticipation. The triumphs and challenges of the past season become a crucible, forging lessons and insights that will shape the team's trajectory in the seasons to come. The pursuit of excellence, a hallmark of Steiner's leadership, remains unwavering.

As the off-season unfolds, Steiner's focus shifts to the planning and preparation for the upcoming challenges. The team's headquarters in Mooresville, North Carolina, buzzes with activity as engineers, mechanics, and strategists collaborate to refine the car, enhance performance, and build on the successes of the previous season. Steiner's vision for the future becomes a guiding beacon, ensuring that every aspect of the team aligns with the pursuit of greatness.

Media engagements continue to be a dynamic aspect of Steiner's role. Reflecting on the highs and lows of the past season, he provides fans and pundits with insights into the team's evolution. The interviews become a platform to articulate the vision for the future, fostering anticipation and excitement for what lies ahead. Steiner's candid communication style maintains the bond between Haas F1 Team and its global audience.

The town of Mooresville, with its ties to motorsport excellence, evolves as a testament to the enduring impact of Haas F1 Team. Steiner's commitment to community engagement and sustainability initiatives solidifies the team's position not just as a racing entity but as a positive force in the lives of those it touches. The legacy extends beyond the racetrack, resonating with the spirit of Mooresville.

The nurturing of young talent within Haas F1 Team takes center stage as emerging drivers continue to prove their mettle. Steiner's commitment to providing a platform for young racers becomes a catalyst for fresh perspectives and innovative approaches. The team's dedication to talent development remains a key pillar in Steiner's strategy for sustained success.

As the calendar turns, the anticipation builds for the upcoming Formula One season. The roar of the engines awaits, and with it, the promise of new narratives, challenges, and triumphs. Steiner's journey, a tapestry woven with passion, resilience, and a commitment to excellence, continues to unfold. The racetrack beckons, and the legacy of Guenther Steiner in the ever-evolving drama of Formula One is destined to be written in the chapters yet to come.

As the new Formula One season dawns, Guenther Steiner and Haas F1 Team stand at the precipice of a fresh chapter in their storied journey. The buzz of anticipation reverberates through the team's headquarters in Mooresville, North Carolina, where Steiner's leadership sets the tone for the challenges and triumphs that lie ahead.

The off-season becomes a canvas for innovation and refinement as Haas F1 Team meticulously fine-tunes its machinery. Steiner's strategic vision takes shape in the form of aerodynamic enhancements, technical upgrades, and a renewed commitment to pushing the boundaries of performance. The team's pursuit of excellence is not just a seasonal goal but a continuous, relentless endeavor.

Media interactions once again thrust Steiner into the spotlight. Press conferences, interviews, and behind-the-scenes glimpses become conduits for sharing the team's evolution. Steiner's authentic communication style resonates, weaving a narrative that transcends the technicalities of Formula One, allowing fans to connect with the human stories and ambitions that unfold within the racing world.

Mooresville transforms into a hub of anticipation as the community rallies behind Haas F1 Team. Steiner's outreach initiatives, educational programs, and sustainability efforts continue to underscore the team's commitment to leaving a positive impact. The town becomes a living testament to the symbiotic relationship between motorsport excellence and community engagement.

The nurturing of young talent remains a focal point as the emerging drivers, guided by Steiner's mentorship, gear up for the challenges of the upcoming season. The team's dedication to fostering the next generation of racing stars solidifies its position as a breeding ground for talent, and Steiner's belief in the potential of youth continues to shape the dynamic roster of Haas F1 Team.

As the engines roar to life on the first race weekend, the legacy of Guenther Steiner enters a new phase. The pursuit of podiums, points, and championships unfolds against the backdrop of the world's most iconic circuits. Steiner's experience becomes a guiding force, steering Haas F1 Team through the twists and turns of the Formula One calendar.

The 2024 season becomes a canvas on which the team's narrative is painted lap by lap, race by race. The victories become not just triumphs for Haas F1 Team but milestones in Steiner's enduring journey in the pinnacle of motorsport. The pursuit of greatness is not just a destination but a journey, and under Steiner's leadership, every race becomes a step forward in that relentless pursuit.

As the checkered flags fall, and the roar of the engines fades, the legacy of Guenther Steiner continues to unfold. Each season becomes a chapter, and the story of Haas F1 Team becomes intertwined with the broader narrative of Formula One. The journey, marked by passion, innovation, and a commitment to excellence, becomes a testament to the enduring allure of the sport and the indomitable spirit of those who dare to push the limits.

The future beckons, promising more exhilarating races, unforeseen challenges, and moments that will etch themselves into the pages of motorsport history. Guenther Steiner, with his steady hand at the helm, leads Haas F1 Team into the next frontier, where the pursuit of greatness knows no bounds. The story continues, and the racetrack awaits its next chapter in the epic tale of Formula One.

As the Formula One circus travels the globe, Guenther Steiner's Haas F1 Team becomes a testament to resilience and adaptability in the face of the ever-evolving motorsport landscape. The 2024 season unfolds as a tapestry of strategic gambles, technical prowess, and human endeavor, with Steiner orchestrating the symphony of engineering and racing talent.

The paddocks, from the glitz of Monaco to the speed temples of Monza, buzz with the energy and anticipation of each race weekend. Steiner, a figure of calm amidst the whirlwind of activity, navigates the complexities of managing a top-tier Formula One team. His decisions on strategy, driver management, and team dynamics are critical, each choice reverberating through the season's outcome.

Throughout the year, Haas F1 Team's headquarters in Mooresville remains a hive of activity. Here, Steiner's influence extends beyond the racetrack. His commitment to technological advancement sees the team pushing the boundaries of simulation and data analysis, striving for every possible edge in a sport where milliseconds separate triumph from obscurity.

Steiner's rapport with the drivers, both seasoned and newcomers, is pivotal. His guidance, often a blend of stern realism and motivational leadership, shapes the psyche and performance of his drivers. The bond between team principal and driver transcends the cockpit, impacting performance, morale, and the collective pursuit of success.

Media engagements continue to keep Steiner in the public eye, his frank and often humorous takes providing a human touch to the high-stakes world of Formula One. His insights offer a window into the inner workings of the sport, endearing him to fans and adding depth to the narrative of each race weekend.

The community in Mooresville and beyond watches with pride as Haas F1 Team, under Steiner's stewardship, represents not just American ingenuity in a predominantly European sport but also the spirit of determination and excellence. The team's community initiatives, championed by Steiner, reinforce this bond, making Haas F1 more than just a team but a beacon in the world of motorsport.

Internally, Steiner cultivates a culture of continuous improvement. His focus on nurturing talent within the team fosters an environment where ideas and innovation are valued. This culture extends to the drivers, mechanics, engineers, and even the administrative staff, all united under Steiner's vision of collective growth and achievement.

As the season reaches its climax, each race becomes a battleground where strategy, skill, and technology converge. Steiner, a master tactician, leverages his years of experience to make split-second decisions that can mean the difference between victory and defeat. The team's successes, as well as its challenges, are shared, with Steiner often serving as the rallying point, the voice of reason in the high-octane world of Formula One racing.

The legacy of Guenther Steiner, intricately woven into the fabric of Haas F1 Team, continues to evolve. As the season concludes and the motorsport world begins to look towards the next year, Steiner's vision for the future becomes clear. It's a vision that encompasses technological innovation, human talent, and a relentless pursuit of excellence.

In the world of Formula One, where the only constant is change, Guenther Steiner stands as a figure of resilience, innovation, and leadership. His journey, far from over, promises more chapters of success, learning, and unyielding passion for the sport. The story of Haas F1 Team, under the stewardship of Steiner, is an ongoing saga of ambition, challenge, and the relentless pursuit of greatness in the fast-paced world of Formula One

Printed in Great Britain
by Amazon